GUITAR
LEARN TO PLAY ANYWHERE & ANYTIME

RON MANUS • L. C. HARNSBERGER

DiY is an interactive multimedia experience—with video and audio demonstrations available for every lesson, example, and song in the book. You can stream or download corresponding media to your computer or mobile device wherever you see ⬇️. Simply follow along in the book, and you will have everything you need.

To access the accompanying media, go to **alfred.com/redeem** and enter the code found on the inside front cover of this book.

Alfred Music
P.O. Box 10003
Van Nuys, CA 91410-0003
alfred.com

ISBN-10: 1-4706-1139-2 (Book & Media)
ISBN-13: 978-1-4706-1139-2 (Book & Media)

Guitar photo courtesy of C.F. Martin & Company
Gears: © iStockphoto / aleksandarvelasevic • Blueprint: © iStockphoto / Branislav

 Alfred Cares. Contents printed on environmentally responsible paper.

CONTENTS
DO IT YOURSELF: GUITAR

THE PARTS OF THE GUITAR
DO IT YOURSELF: GUITAR

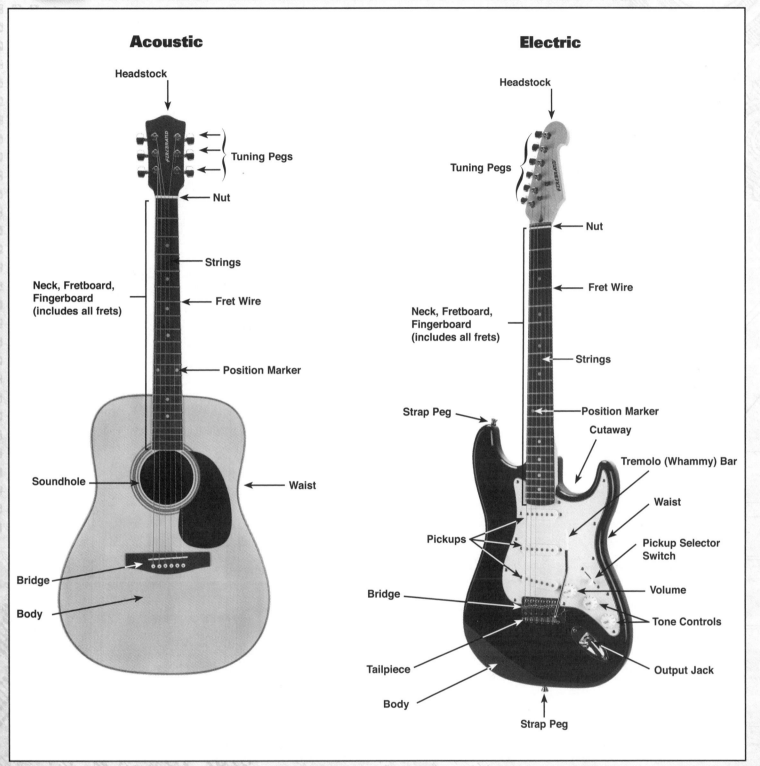

Acoustic

- Headstock
- Tuning Pegs
- Nut
- Strings
- Neck, Fretboard, Fingerboard (includes all frets)
- Fret Wire
- Position Marker
- Soundhole
- Waist
- Bridge
- Body

Electric

- Headstock
- Tuning Pegs
- Nut
- Fret Wire
- Neck, Fretboard, Fingerboard (includes all frets)
- Strings
- Position Marker
- Strap Peg
- Cutaway
- Tremolo (Whammy) Bar
- Waist
- Pickup Selector Switch
- Pickups
- Volume
- Bridge
- Tone Controls
- Tailpiece
- Output Jack
- Body
- Strap Peg

Steel Strings and Nylon Strings

Steel strings are found on both acoustic and electric guitars. They have a bright and brassy sound.

Nylon strings are usually found on classical and flamenco guitars. They have a mellow, delicate sound. Nylon strings are often easier for beginners to play because they are easier on the fingers than steel strings.

HOW TO HOLD YOUR GUITAR

DO IT YOURSELF: GUITAR

Below are three ways to hold your guitar.
Pick the one that is most comfortable for you.

When playing, keep your left wrist away from the fingerboard. This will allow your fingers to be in a better position to finger the chords. Press your fingers firmly, but make certain they do not touch the neighboring strings.

Sitting.

Sitting with legs crossed.

Standing with strap.

THE RIGHT HAND
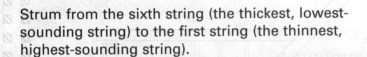

To *strum* means to play the strings with your right hand by brushing quickly across them. There are two common ways of strumming the strings. One is with a pick, and the other is with your fingers.

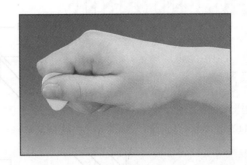

Strumming with a Pick
Hold the pick between your thumb and index finger. Hold it firmly, but don't squeeze it too hard.

Strum from the sixth string (the thickest, lowest-sounding string) to the first string (the thinnest, highest-sounding string).

Start near the thickest string.

Move mostly your wrist, not just your arm. Finish near the thinnest string.

Important:
Strum by mostly moving your wrist, not just your arm. Use as little motion as possible. Start as close to the *top string* as you can, and never let your hand move past the edge of the guitar.

Strumming with Your Fingers
First, decide if you feel more comfortable strumming with the side of your thumb or the nail of your index finger. The strumming motion is the same with the thumb or finger as it is when using the pick. Strum from the sixth string (the thickest, lowest-sounding string) to the first string (the thinnest, highest-sounding string)

Strumming with the thumb.

Strumming with the index finger.

Here is a great exercise to get used to strumming.

LET'S STRUM
Strum all six strings slowly and evenly. Count your strums out loud as you play. Repeat this exercise until you feel comfortable strumming the strings.

	strum	strum	strum	strum	strum	strum	strum	strum
	/	/	/	/	/	/	/	/
Count:	1	2	3	4	5	6	7	8

Proper Left-Hand Position

Learning to use your left-hand fingers starts with a good hand position. Place your hand so your thumb rests comfortably in the middle of the back of the neck. Position your fingers on the front of the neck as if you are gently squeezing a ball between them and your thumb. Keep your elbow in and your fingers curved.

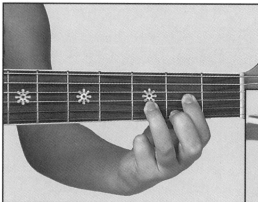

Keep elbow in and fingers curved.

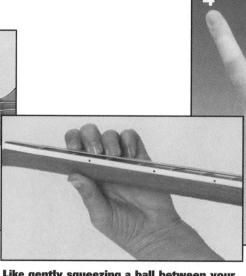

Like gently squeezing a ball between your fingertips and thumb.

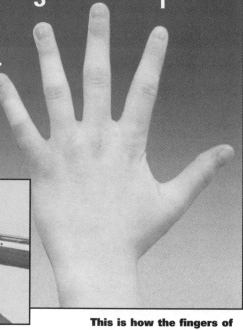

This is how the fingers of the left hand are numbered.

Placing a Finger on a String

When you press a string with a left-hand finger, make sure you press firmly with the tip of your finger and as close to the fret wire as you can without actually being right on it. Short fingernails are important! This will create a clean, bright tone.

RIGHT
Finger presses the string down near the fret without actually being on it.

WRONG
Finger is too far from fret wire; tone is "buzzy" and indefinite.

WRONG
Finger is on top of fret wire; tone is muffled and unclear.

TUNING YOUR GUITAR
DO IT YOURSELF: GUITAR

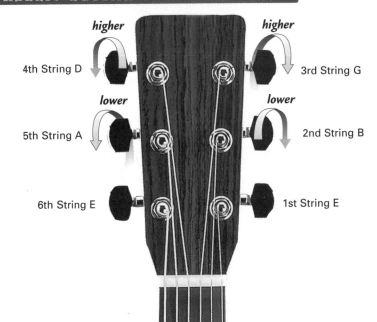

First, make sure your strings are wound properly around the tuning pegs. They should go from the inside to the outside as illustrated to the right. Some guitars have all six tuning pegs on the same side of the headstock. If this is the case, make sure all six strings are wound the same way, from the inside out.

Turning a tuning peg clockwise makes the pitch lower. Turning a tuning peg counterclockwise makes the pitch higher. Be sure not to tune the strings too high because they could break.

Important:

Always remember that the thinnest, highest-sounding string, the one closest to the floor, is the first string. The thickest, lowest-sounding string, the one closest to the ceiling, is the sixth string. When guitarists say "the highest string," they are referring to the highest-sounding string.

Tuning to the Online Media

When tuning while watching the online media, listen to the directions and match each of your guitar's strings to the corresponding pitches on the online media.

Tuning the Guitar to Itself

When your sixth string is in tune, you can tune the rest of the strings using the guitar alone. First, tune the sixth string to E on the piano:

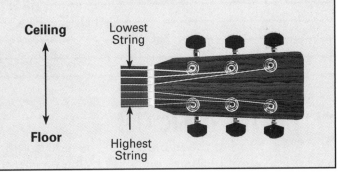

Then, follow the instructions below to get the guitar in tune.

Press 5th fret of 6th string to get pitch of 5th string (A).

Press 5th fret of 5th string to get pitch of 4th string (D).

Press 5th fret of 4th string to get pitch of 3rd string (G).

Press 4th fret of 3rd string to get pitch of 2nd string (B).

Press 5th fret of 2nd string to get pitch of 1st string (E).

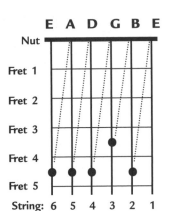

Pitch Pipes and Electronic Tuners

If you don't have a piano available, consider buying an electronic tuner or pitch pipe. There are many types available, and a salesperson at your local music store can help you decide which is best for you.

THE BASICS OF READING MUSIC

DO IT YOURSELF: GUITAR

Musical sounds are indicated by symbols called *notes.* Their time value is determined by their color (white or black) and by stems or flags attached to the note.

The Staff

The notes are named after the first seven letters of the alphabet (A–G), which are repeated to embrace the entire range of musical sound. The name and pitch of a note are determined by the note's position on the *staff,* which is made up of five horizontal lines and four spaces between.

```
——————————————— 5th LINE ———————————————
                                                    4th SPACE
——————————— 4th LINE ———————————
                                              3rd SPACE
——————— 3rd LINE ———————
                                          2nd SPACE
——— 2nd LINE ———
                                    1st SPACE
— 1st LINE —
```

The Treble Clef

During the evolution of musical notation, the staff had from 2 to 20 lines, and symbols were invented to locate certain lines and the pitch of the note on that line. These symbols were called *clefs.*

Music for the guitar is written in the *G clef or treble clef.* Originally the Gothic letter G was used on a four-line staff to establish the pitch of G.

This grew into the modern symbol we use today:

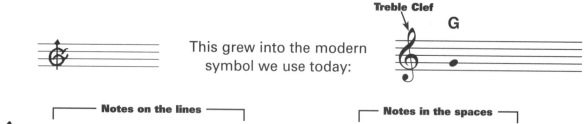

Notes on the lines   E G B D F

Notes in the spaces   F A C E

Measures (Bars)

Music is also divided into equal parts called *measures,* or *bars.* One measure is divided from another by a *bar line:*

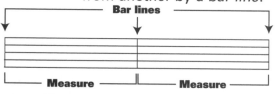

Bar lines

Measure   Measure

The Quarter Note

A quarter note equals one count.

Reading TAB

All the music in this book is written two ways: in standard music notation and in *TAB*. Below each standard music staff you'll find a six-line TAB staff. Each line represents a string of the guitar, with the highest, thinnest string at the top and the lowest, thickest string at the bottom.

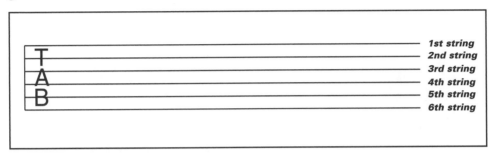

Numbers placed on the TAB lines tell you which fret to play. A zero means to play the string open (not fingered).

1st string	2nd string	3rd string	4th string
3rd fret	1st fret	open	2nd fret

Numbers placed one on top of the other are played at the same time.

1st string, open 2nd string, 1st fret	2nd, 3rd, and 4th strings open	1st string, 1st fret and three open strings	A five-note C chord

By glancing at the TAB, you can immediately tell where to play a note. Although you can't tell exactly what the rhythm is from the TAB, the horizontal spacing of the numbers gives you a strong hint about how long or short the notes are to be played.

How to Read Chord Diagrams

Fingering diagrams show where to place the fingers of your left hand. Strings that are not played are shown with a dashed line. The finger that is to be pressed down is shown as a circle with a number in it. The number indicates which finger is used. The diagram at the right shows the first finger on the first fret.

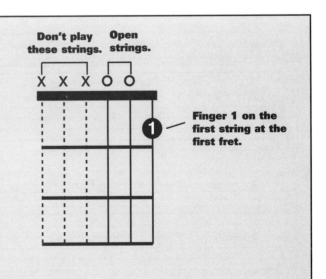

NOTES ON THE FIRST STRING E
DO IT YOURSELF: GUITAR

OPEN STRING
(not fingered)

1st FRET

3rd FRET

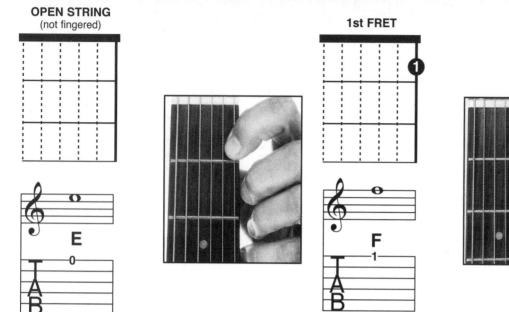

E

F

G

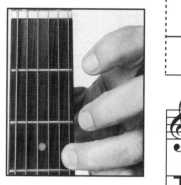

Play this example slowly and evenly. Use down-strokes for all the music in this book.

Go to the next line without stopping.

A *double bar line* indicates the end of a piece.

PLAYING E, F, AND G ON MY EXTRA FINE GUITAR

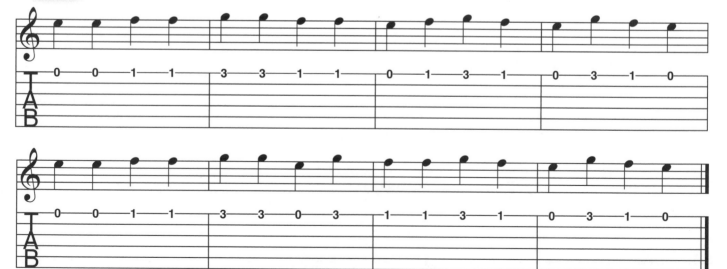

EXTRA CREDIT

Make sure to place your left-hand fingers as close to the fret wires as possible without touching them. When you play the F on the 1st fret and follow it with the G on the 3rd fret, keep the first finger down. You will only hear the G, but when you go back to the F, it will sound smooth.

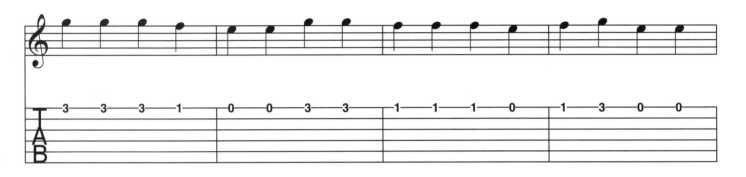

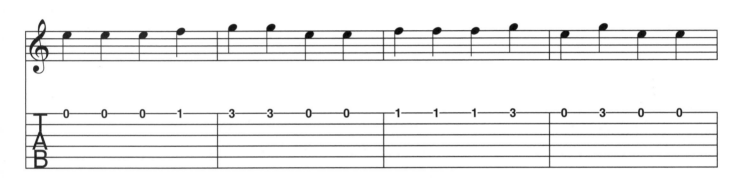

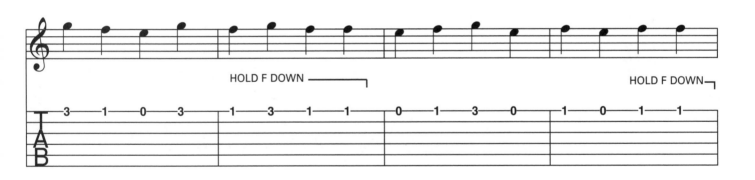

COUNTING TIME

Four Kinds of Notes

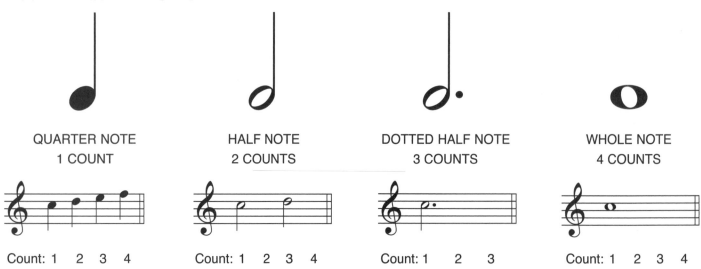

QUARTER NOTE
1 COUNT

Count: 1 2 3 4

HALF NOTE
2 COUNTS

Count: 1 2 3 4

DOTTED HALF NOTE
3 COUNTS

Count: 1   2   3

WHOLE NOTE
4 COUNTS

Count: 1 2 3 4

Time Signatures

Each piece of music has numbers at the beginning called a *time signature.* These numbers tell us how to count time.

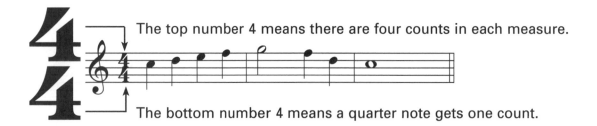

The top number 4 means there are four counts in each measure.

The bottom number 4 means a quarter note gets one count.

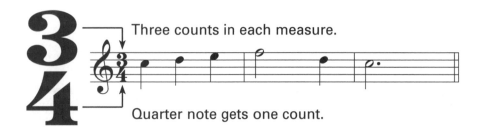

Three counts in each measure.

Quarter note gets one count.

IMPORTANT: Fill in the missing time signatures of the songs already learned.

NOTES ON THE SECOND STRING B

DO IT YOURSELF: GUITAR

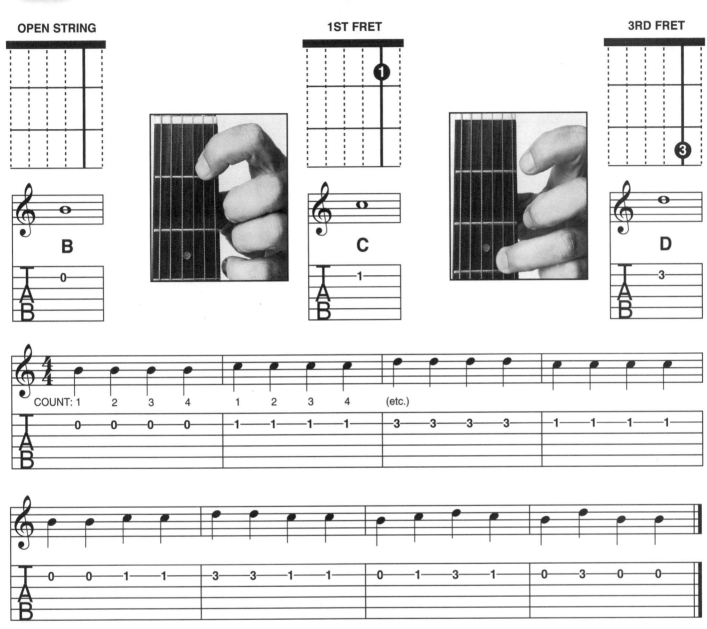

JAMMIN' ON TWO STRINGS

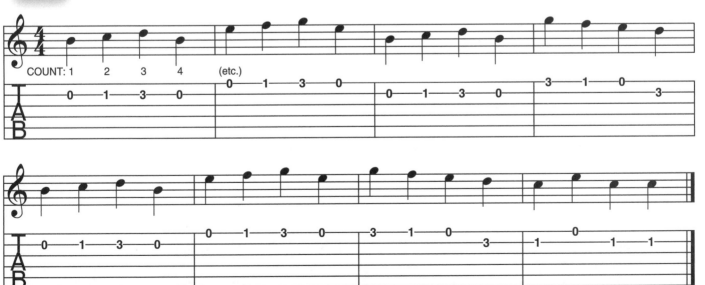

BEAUTIFUL BROWN EYES

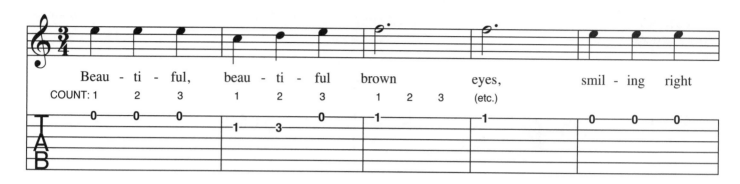

Beau - ti - ful, beau - ti - ful brown eyes, smil - ing right

COUNT: 1   2   3   1   2   3   1   2   3   (etc.)

in - to my heart. But now where are those beau - ti - ful

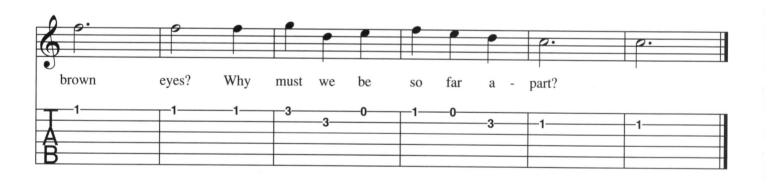

brown eyes? Why must we be so far a - part?

ROCKIN' GUITAR

Letters called *chord symbols* that are placed above each staff may be used for a duet. Either have a friend or teacher play the chords while you play the notes, or play along with the audio tracks online. Many of the tunes in the rest of this book include chords for duets.

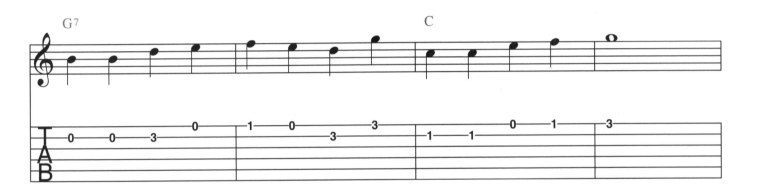

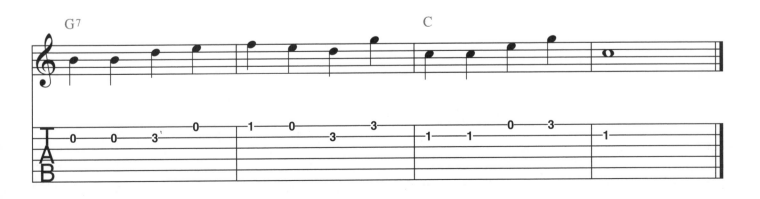

JINGLE BELLS

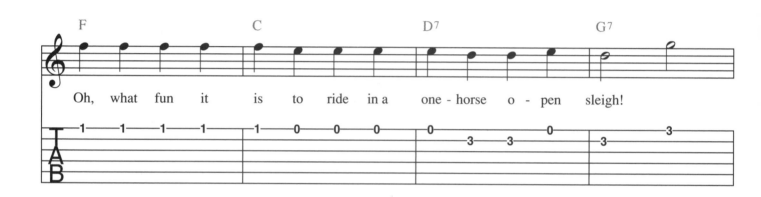

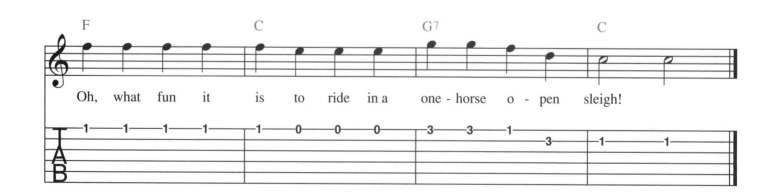

NOTES ON THE THIRD STRING G
DO IT YOURSELF: GUITAR

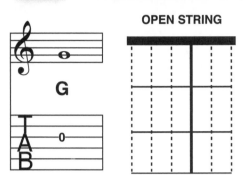

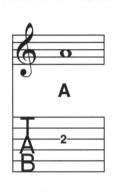

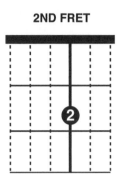

JAMMIN' ON THREE STRINGS

18

LARGO
from the *New World Symphony*

Dvořák

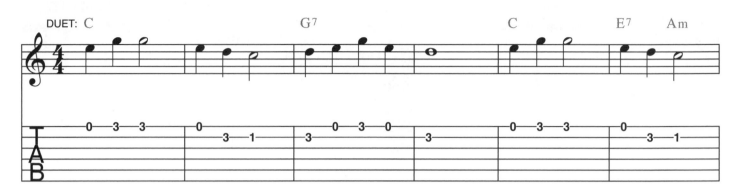

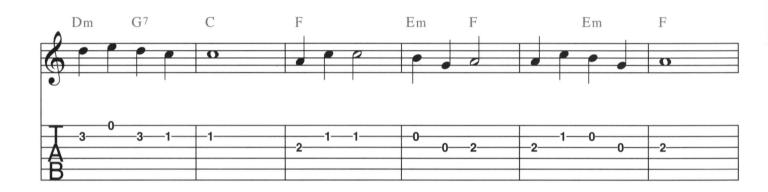

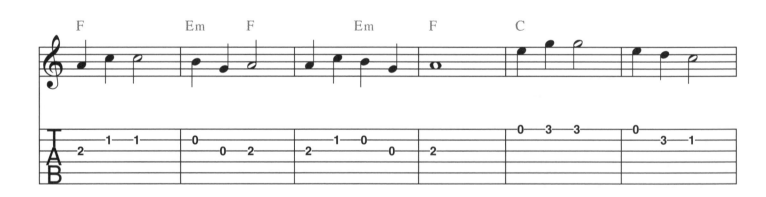

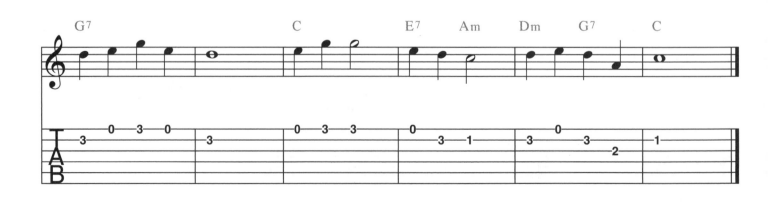

REPEAT SIGNS
DO IT YOURSELF: GUITAR

"Aura Lee" is an old American folk song that was later recorded by Elvis Presley and called "Love Me Tender." This music uses *repeat signs.* The double dots inside the double bars tell you that everything between those double bars is to be repeated.

 AURA LEE

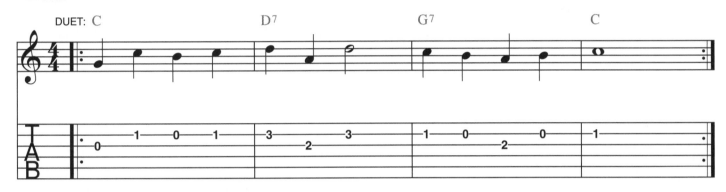

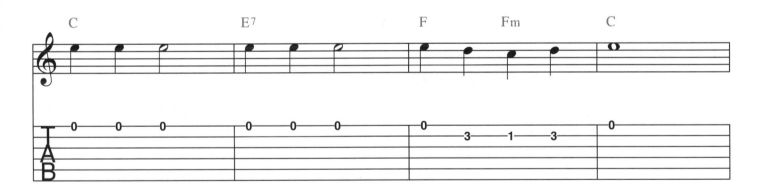

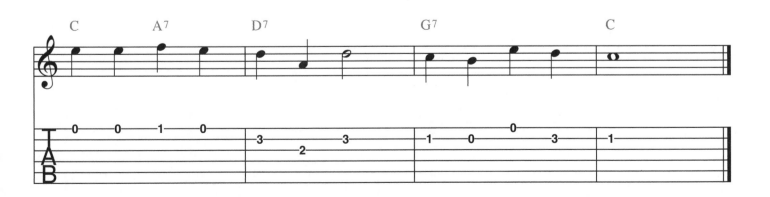

CHORDS
DO IT YOURSELF: GUITAR

A *chord* is a combination of three or more notes played at the same time. All the notes are connected by a stem unless they are whole notes, which have no stem. The stems can go either up or down, depending on where notes are located on the staff.

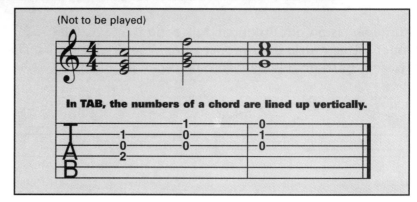

Two-Note Exercise

This exercise will get you used to playing two notes at a time—open B and open E. Play both strings together with one down-stroke.

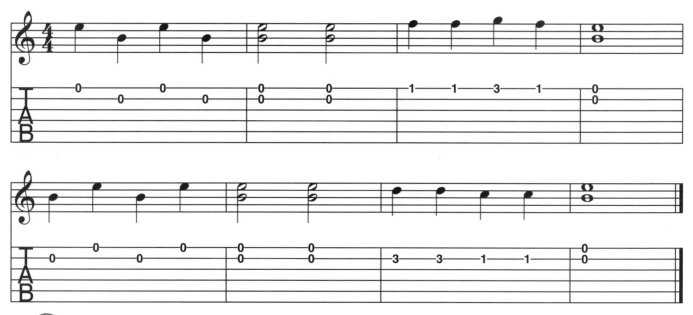

Three-Note Chord Exercise

This is the first time you are playing three-note chords. All the chords in this exercise are made up of the open G, B, and E strings. Play it with your wrist free and relaxed. Remember to keep your eyes on the notes and not your hands.

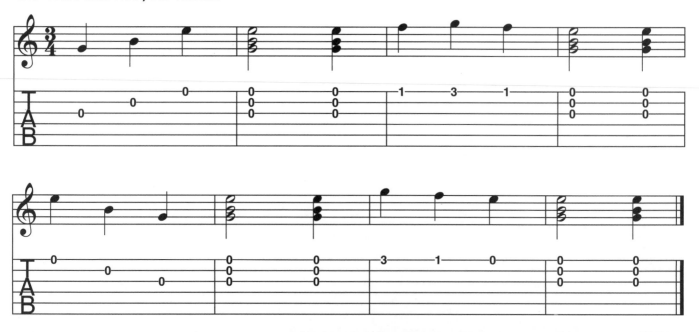

THREE-STRING C CHORD
DO IT YOURSELF: GUITAR

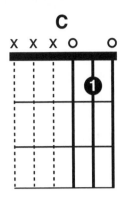

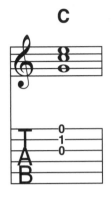

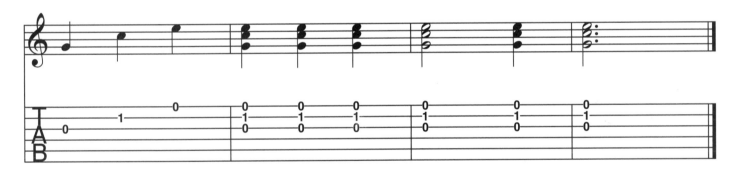

One of the giants of rock 'n' roll, from his first records with The Beatles through his successful solo career, John Lennon played a major role in shaping pop music into what it is today. His combination of graceful melodies, unusual chord progressions and literate, sometimes biting, lyrics set a new standard for songwriting that continues to inspire fans around the world.

Photo: Astrid Kichherr courtesy Capitol Records

The Quarter Rest

It tells you to be silent for one count.

To make the rest very clear, stop the sound of the strings by touching the strings lightly with the heel of your right hand.

ODE TO JOY
Theme from *Beethoven's Ninth Symphony*

Beethoven

COUNT: 1   2   3   (4)

THREE-STRING G7 CHORD

DO IT YOURSELF: GUITAR

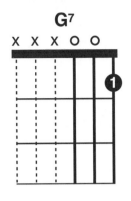

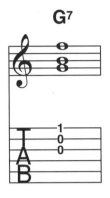

LOVE SOMEBODY

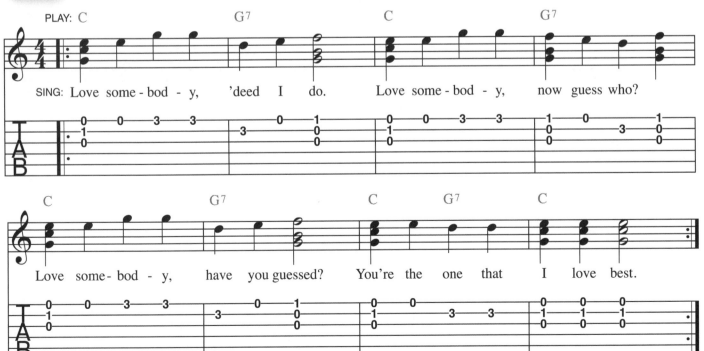

PLAY: C   G7   C   G7

SING: Love some - bod - y,   'deed I do.   Love some - bod - y,   now guess who?

C   G7   C   G7   C

Love some - bod - y,   have you guessed?   You're the one that   I love best.

JAMMIN' WITH TWO CHORDS

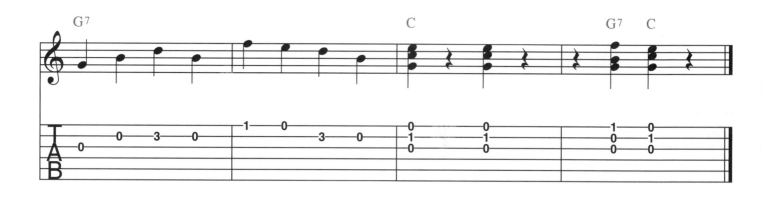

Pete Townshend exploded onto the popular music scene with the influential English group The Who. His innovative guitar techniques include the use of feedback, smashing instruments on stage, and his trademark "windmill" strumming. Pete took rock songwriting to a new level with the landmark rock operas *Tommy* and *Quadrophenia*.

Photo: Neil Zlozower/atlasicons.com

THREE-STRING G CHORD
DO IT YOURSELF: GUITAR

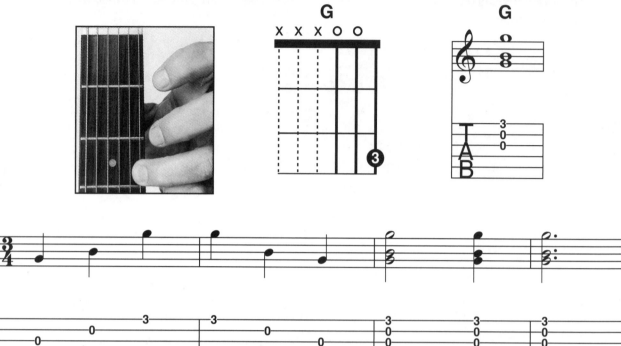

Texas guitarist Stevie Ray Vaughan brought the blues to an entire generation of music lovers and was admired by the likes of Eric Clapton, David Bowie, and Buddy Guy for his extraordinary skill. Tragically, a plane crash claimed the life of this celebrated guitar legend in 1990.

Photo: Robert Knight

SHE'LL BE COMIN' 'ROUND THE MOUNTAIN

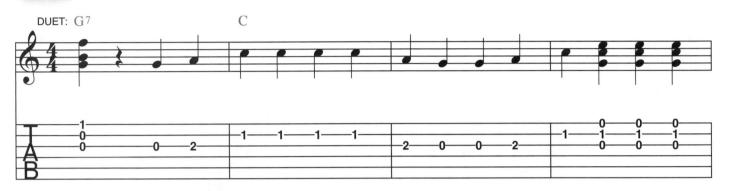

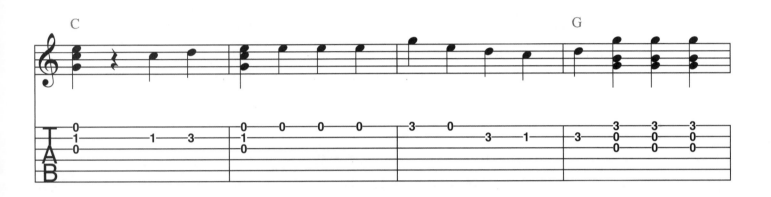

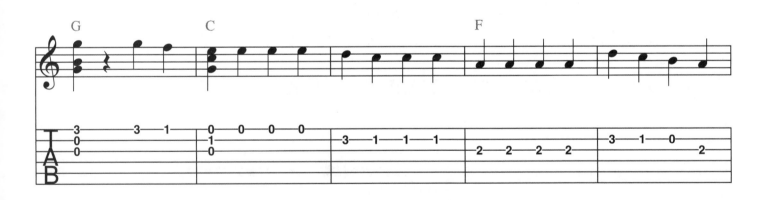

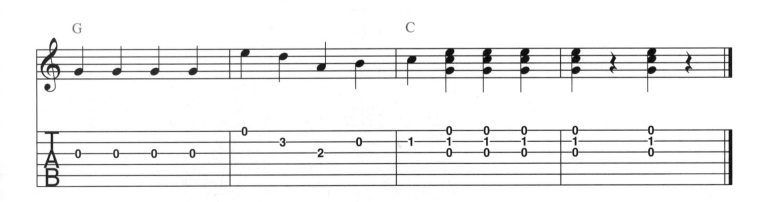

NOTES ON THE FOURTH STRING D

DO IT YOURSELF: GUITAR

OPEN STRING **2ND FRET** **3RD FRET**

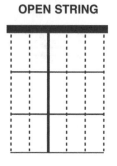
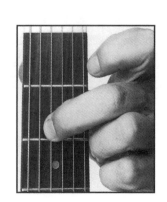
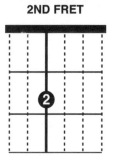

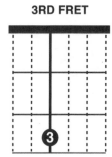

D   E   F

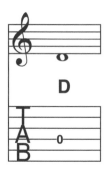
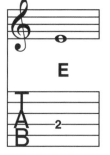
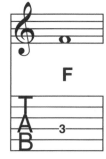

 ## OLD MACDONALD HAD A FARM

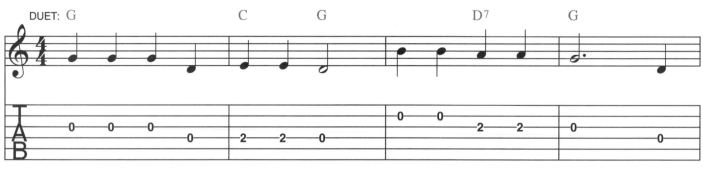

REUBEN REUBEN

"Reuben Reuben" uses a *fermata* (⌒), which is also called a *hold sign* or *pause sign*. This sign tells you to lengthen the value of the note (usually twice its normal value).

C BLUES

C stands for *common time*, which is the same as ⁴⁄₄ time.

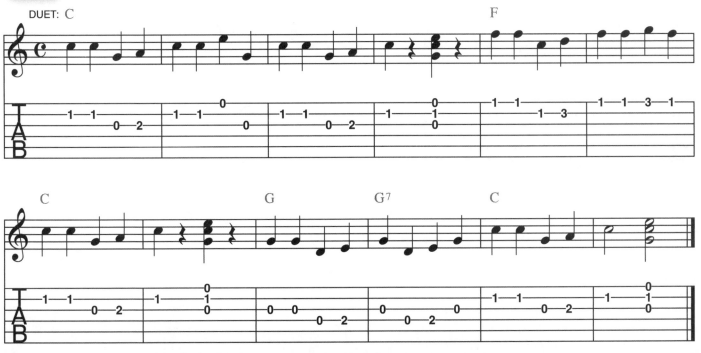

Now that you are getting better at playing chords, here is a song that will be lots of fun to play. In "Daisy Bell," you will be going from one note, to two notes, to three notes.

 DAISY BELL

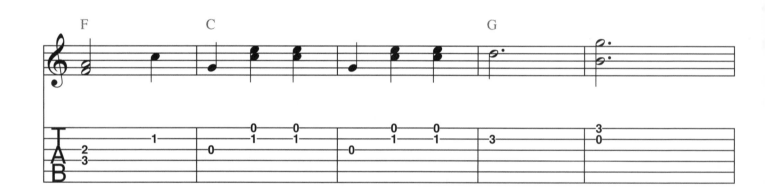

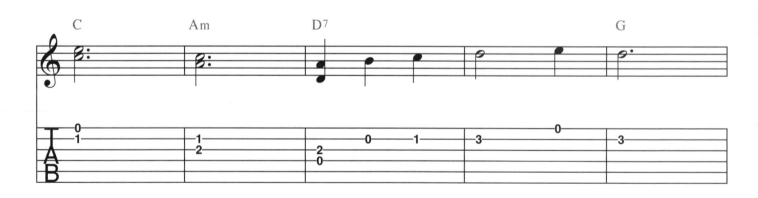

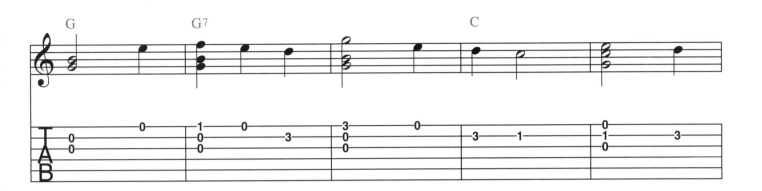

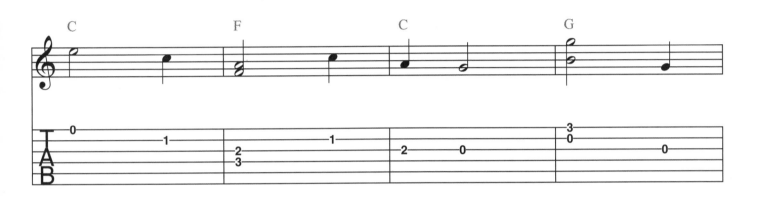

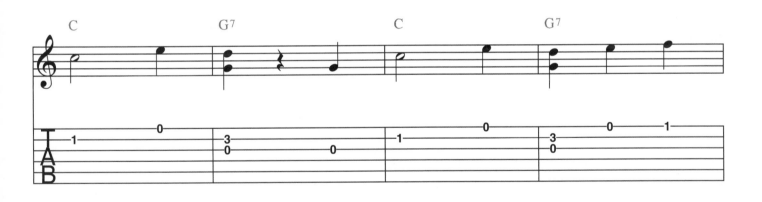

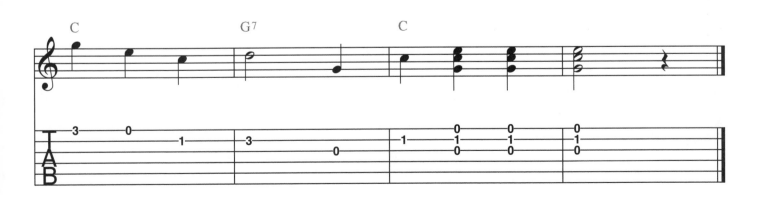

FOUR-STRING G & G7 CHORDS

G

G7

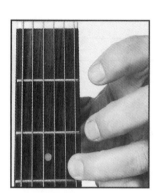

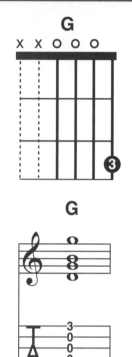

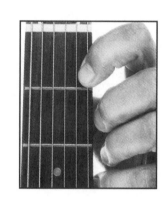

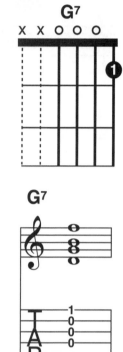

Although these new chords have the same names as chords you have already learned, they use four notes and sound more full.

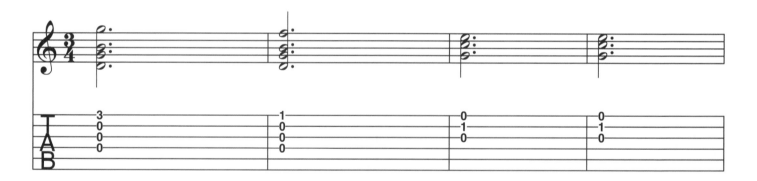

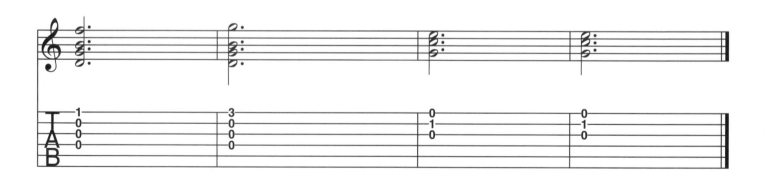

ROCK ME MOZART!

Mozart

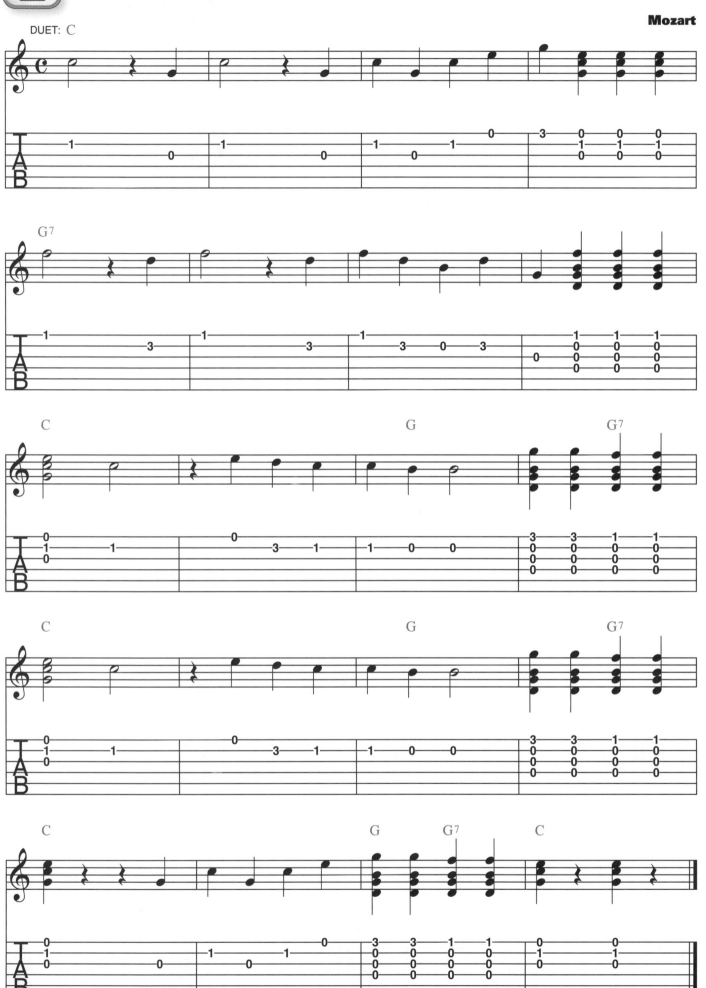

NOTES ON THE FIFTH STRING A
DO IT YOURSELF: GUITAR

OPEN STRING

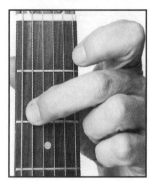

2ND FRET

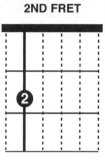

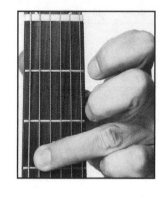

3RD FRET

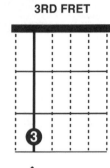

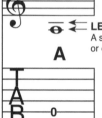

LEDGER LINES
A short line that extends the staff upwards or downwards is called a *ledger* line.

A

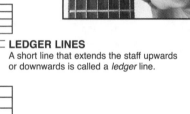

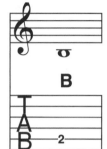

B

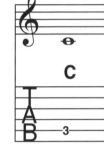

C

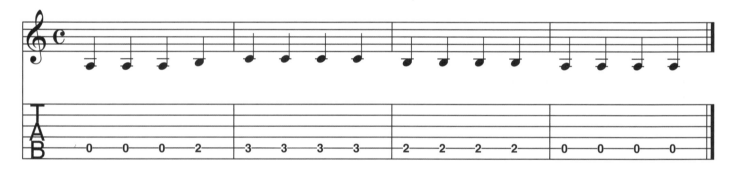

 VOLGA BOATMEN

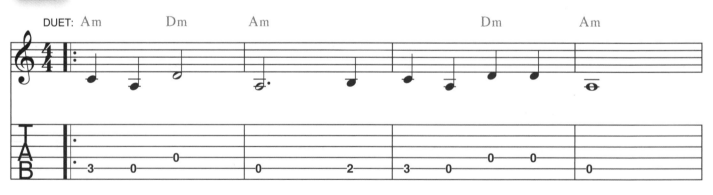

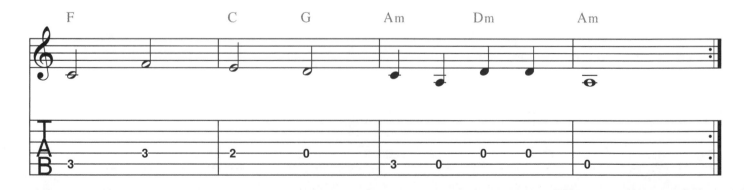

A MINOR BOOGIE

DUET: Am

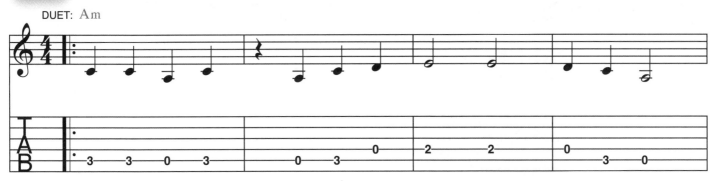

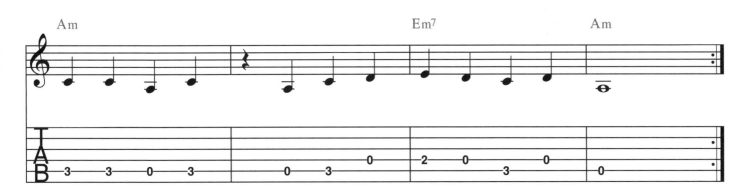

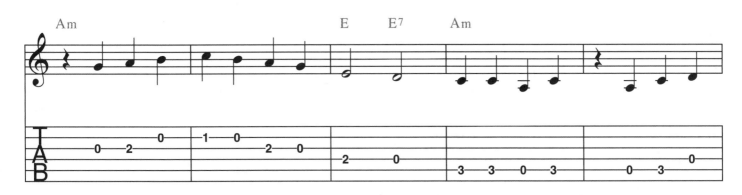

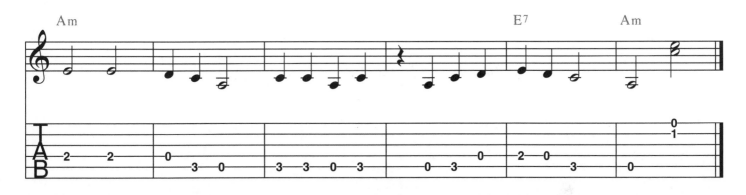

HIGH A
DO IT YOURSELF: GUITAR

 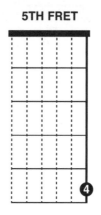 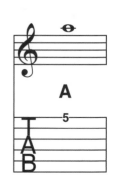

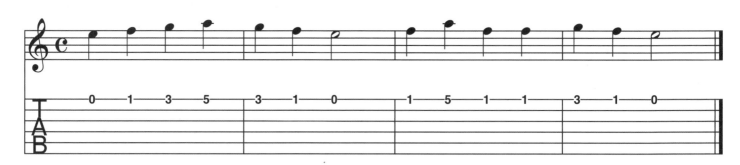

BACK IN RUSSIA

INCOMPLETE MEASURES
DO IT YOURSELF: GUITAR

Not all pieces of music begin on the first beat.

Sometimes, music begins with an incomplete measure called a *pickup*.

If the pickup is one beat, the last measure will only have three beats in $\frac{4}{4}$, or two beats in $\frac{3}{4}$.

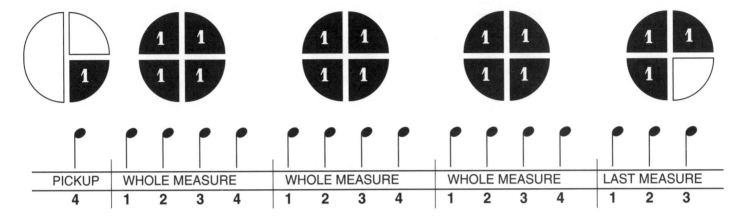

 ## A-TISKET, A-TASKET

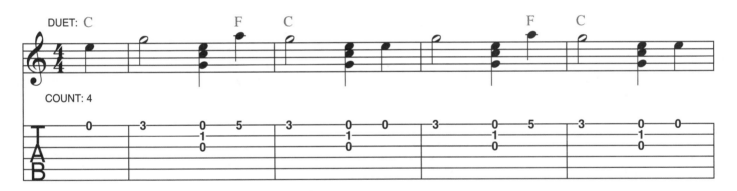

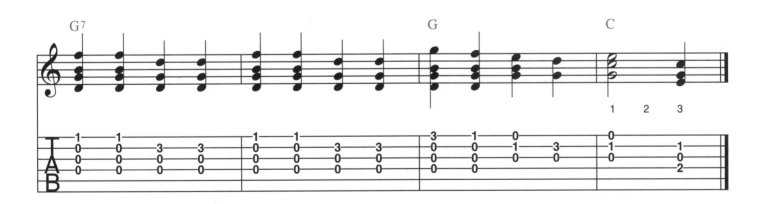

THE YELLOW ROSE OF TEXAS

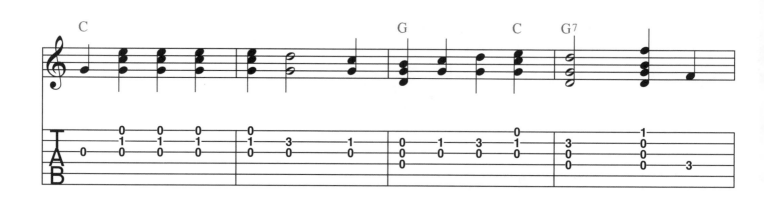

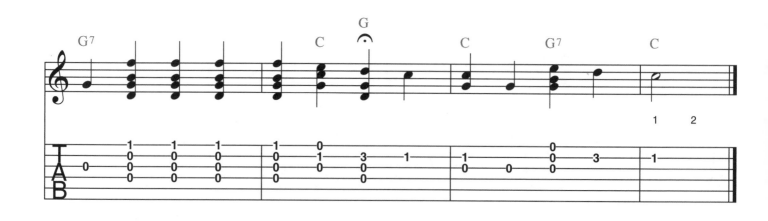

NOTES ON THE SIXTH STRING E

DO IT YOURSELF: GUITAR

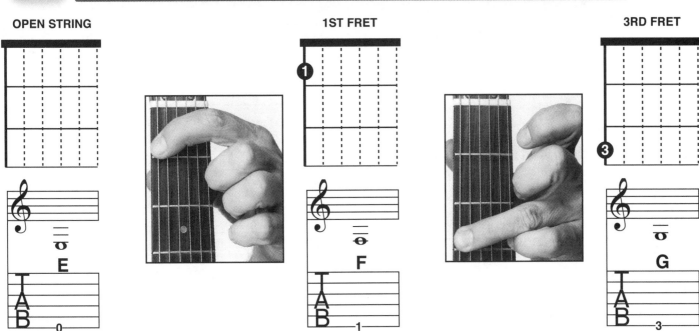

OPEN STRING — E — TAB: 0

1ST FRET — F — TAB: 1

3RD FRET — G — TAB: 3

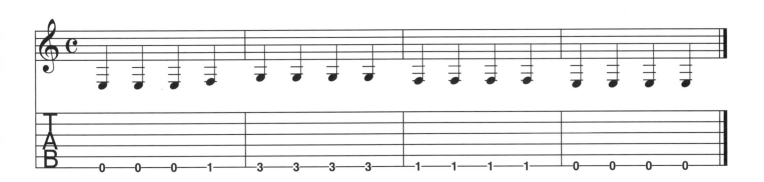

TAB: 0 — 0 — 0 — 1 | 3 — 3 — 3 — 3 | 1 — 1 — 1 — 1 | 0 — 0 — 0 — 0

All the Notes You've Learned So Far

FRETS: 0 1 3 | 0 2 3 | 0 2 3 | 0 2 | 0 1 3 | 0 1 3 5

E F G A B C D E F G A B C D E F G A

TAB:
0 1 3
0 2 3
0 2
0 1 3
0 1 3 5

TEMPO SIGNS
DO IT YOURSELF: GUITAR

A *tempo* sign tells you how fast to play music.

The three most common tempo signs:
Andante (SLOW)
Moderato (MODERATELY)
Allegro (FAST)

THREE-TEMPO ROCK

Play three times: 1st time Andante, 2nd time Moderato, 3rd time Allegro.

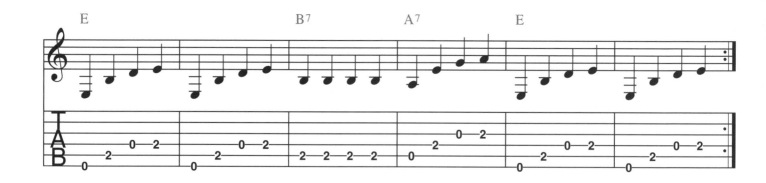

THEME FROM CARMEN

Andante

Bizet

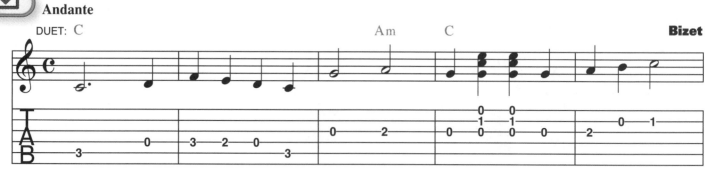

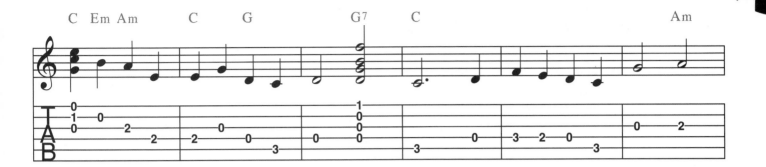

Led Zeppelin remains one of the most influential rock groups of all time, and guitarist Jimmy Page is a major reason why. His pioneering use of scales, as well as his unique blending of classical and blues elements is still widely imitated.

Photo: Robert Knight

BASS-CHORD ACCOMPANIMENT
DO IT YOURSELF: GUITAR

A popular style of playing chord accompaniments in $\frac{4}{4}$ time breaks the chord into two parts: a single bass note followed by a chord made up of the remaining notes. On the 1st beat, play only the lowest note (called the *bass note).* Then play the rest of the chord (usually the three highest strings) on the 2nd, 3rd, and 4th beats. The complete pattern is called **bass-chord-chord-chord.**

Pattern

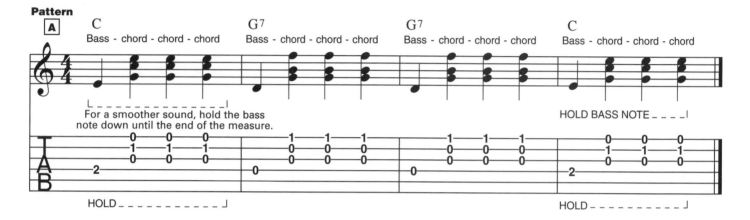

Another style of playing chord accompaniments in $\frac{4}{4}$ time uses a bass note on the 1st and 3rd beats and three-string chords on the 2nd and 4th beats. This is called **bass-chord-bass-chord.**

Pattern

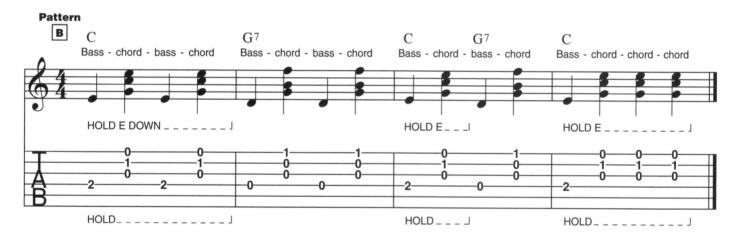

This style of playing chord accompaniments can be adapted to $\frac{3}{4}$ time by playing a bass note on the 1st beat and three-string chords on the 2nd and 3rd beats. This is called **bass-chord-chord.**

Pattern

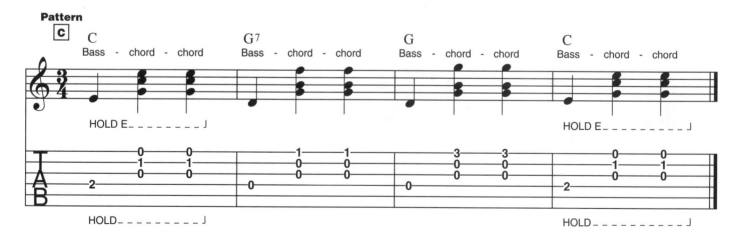

CAN-CAN (DUET)

This famous melody is from the opera *Orpheus in the Underworld* by Jacques Offenbach. You should learn this two different ways: First, play the solo part as written. Second, have a friend or teacher play the solo part, or listen to the online media recording while you play a chord accompaniment using either pattern A or B from page 42.

Offenbach

DYNAMICS
DO IT YOURSELF: GUITAR

Symbols that show how soft or loud to play are called *dynamics.* These symbols come from Italian words. The four most common dynamics are shown here:

 *(piano)* SOFT

 *(mezzo-forte)* MODERATELY LOUD

 (forte) LOUD

 *(fortissimo)* VERY LOUD

 ## THEME FROM BEETHOVEN'S FIFTH SYMPHONY

Beethoven

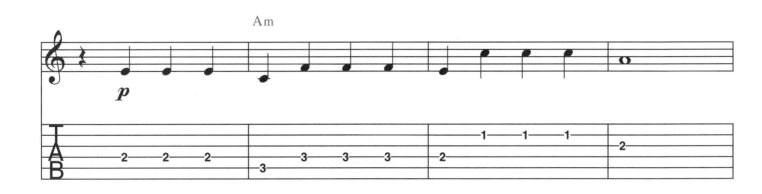

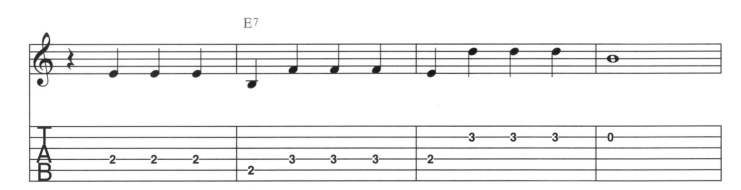

* N.C. means that no chord is played until the next chord symbol.

HALF & WHOLE RESTS

DO IT YOURSELF: GUITAR

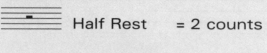

An easy way to remember the difference between the half and whole rest is to think of the whole rest as being longer (or heavier) and so hangs below the line. The half rest is shorter (or lighter) and so sits on top of the line.

Half Rest = 2 counts

Whole Rest = 4 counts in $\frac{4}{4}$ time } for a whole

= 3 counts in $\frac{3}{4}$ time } measure

GIVE IT A REST

Allegro moderato (Moderate rock 'n' roll) *

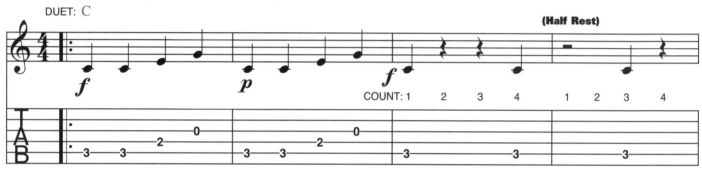

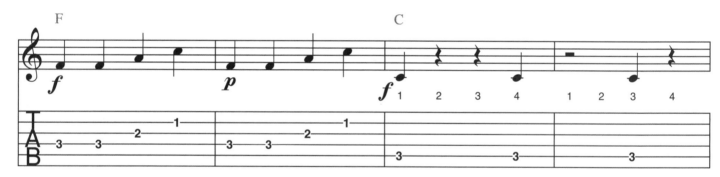

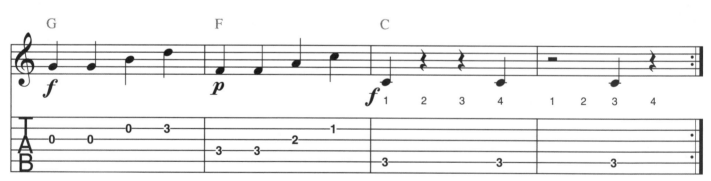

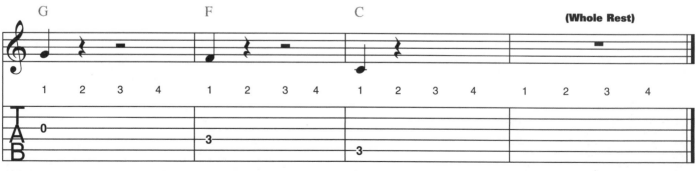

* Allegro moderato is played moderately fast.

FOUR-STRING C CHORD
DO IT YOURSELF: GUITAR

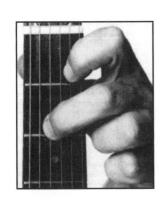
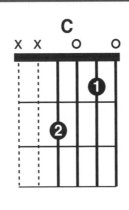
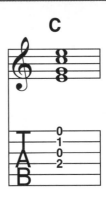

WHEN THE SAINTS GO MARCHING IN

Guitar Fingerboard Chart
Frets 1–12

STRINGS

	6th	5th	4th	3rd	2nd	1st
	E	A	D	G	B	E

FRETS	6th	5th	4th	3rd	2nd	1st
Open	E	A	D	G	B	E
1st Fret	F	A#/Bb	D#/Eb	G#/Ab	C	F
2nd Fret	F#/Gb	B	E	A	C#/Db	F#/Gb
3rd Fret	G	C	F	A#/Bb	D	G
4th Fret	G#/Ab	C#/Db	F#/Gb	B	D#/Eb	G#/Ab
5th Fret	A	D	G	C	E	A
6th Fret	A#/Bb	D#/Eb	G#/Ab	C#/Db	F	A#/Bb
7th Fret	B	E	A	D	F#/Gb	B
8th Fret	C	F	A#/Bb	D#/Eb	G	C
9th Fret	C#/Db	F#/Gb	B	E	G#/Ab	C#/Db
10th Fret	D	G	C	F	A	D
11th Fret	D#/Eb	G#/Ab	C#/Db	F#/Gb	A#/Bb	D#/Eb
12th Fret	E	A	D	G	B	E